At the back of this Book:
Tennessee Reading and Writing Accomplishments

Reading STREET

Tennessee

Program Authors

Peter Afflerbach

Camille Blachowicz

Candy Dawson Boyd

Wendy Cheyney

Connie Juel

Edward Kame'enui

Donald Leu

Jeanne Paratore

P. David Pearson

Sam Sebesta

Deborah Simmons

Sharon Vaughn

Susan Watts-Taffe

Karen Kring Wixson

PEARSON
Scott Foresman

Editorial Offices: Glenview, Illinois • Parsippany, New Jersey • New York, New York
Sales Offices: Boston, Massachusetts • Duluth, Georgia • Glenview, Illinois
Coppell, Texas • Sacramento, California • Mesa, Arizona

We dedicate Reading Street to
Peter Jovanovich.

His wisdom, courage,
and passion for education
are an inspiration to us all.

About the Cover Artist

Daniel Moreton lives in New York City, where he uses his computer to create illustrations for books. When he is not working, Daniel enjoys cooking, watching movies, and traveling. On a trip to Mexico, Daniel was inspired by all of the bright colors around him. He likes to use those colors in his art.

ISBN: 0-328-26116-5

2 3 4 5 6 7 8 9 10 V063 15 14 13 12 11 10 09 08 07

Dear Tennessee Reader,

Are you enjoying your travels along *Scott Foresman Reading Street?* What new skills have you learned to help you read and understand new things? What strategies have helped you smooth out the "bumps in the road" as you read?

As you continue along *Scott Foresman Reading Street,* you will read about people in communities at home, in school, and in neighborhoods. You will also read about communities in nature. So, buckle your seat belt and enjoy the trip!

Sincerely,
The Authors

What is a community?

People in Communities

Unit Opener. 8

Let's Talk About People in Communities. 10

Words to Read. 12

animal fantasy

Max and Ruby: A Big Fish for Max 14

written and designed by Rosemary Wells
illustrated by Jody Wheeler

photo essay/social studies

At Home. 30

Language Arts: Nouns 34

Let's Talk About People in Communities 36

Words to Read 38

realistic fiction/social studies
The Farmer in the Hat 40
by Pat Cummings

expository nonfiction/social studies
Helping Hands at 4-H 56
by Lindy Russell

Language Arts: Proper Nouns 62

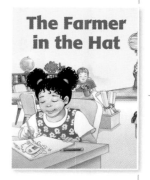

Let's Talk About People in Communities 64

Words to Read 66

expository nonfiction/social studies
Who Works Here? 68
by Melissa Blackwell Burke
illustrated by Tim Spransy

map/social studies
Neighborhood Map 80

Language Arts: Special Titles 82

Communities in Nature

Let's Talk About Communities in Nature. **84**

Words to Read. **86**

fiction/science
The Big Circle **88**
by Eric Kimmel
illustrated by Richard Bernal

newspaper article/social studies
Class Paper **106**

Language Arts: Days, Months, and Holidays **110**

Let's Talk About Communities in Nature. **112**

Words to Read. **114**

expository nonfiction/science
Life in the Forest **116**
by Claire Daniel

expository nonfiction/science
A Mangrove Forest **132**
by Terry Lynk
illustrated by Russell Farrell

Language Arts: One and More Than One **136**

Let's Talk About Communities in Nature. **138**

Words to Read. **140**

expository nonfiction/science
Honey Bees 142

by Jesús Cervantes

illustrated by Tom Leonard

poetry
The Ants Go Marching 160

illustrated by Norman Gorbaty

Language Arts: Nouns in Sentences **162**

Unit Wrap-Up **164**

Pictionary **166**

Tested Words List **174**

Communities

What is a community?

Max and Ruby:
A Big Fish for Max

connect to
SOCIAL STUDIES

A rabbit family has
fun together.

ANIMAL FANTASY

The Farmer
in the Hat

connect to
SOCIAL STUDIES

Students work together
in school.

REALISTIC FICTION

Who Works Here?

connect to
SOCIAL STUDIES

Many people work
in a community.

EXPOSITORY NONFICTION

The Big Circle

connect to
SCIENCE

Animals work together to
keep one another safe.

FICTION

Life in the Forest

connect to
SCIENCE

Plants and animals live
together in a forest.

EXPOSITORY NONFICTION

Honey Bees

connect to
SCIENCE

Bees are insects that
live in communities.

EXPOSITORY NONFICTION

Let's Talk About

People in Communities

Words to Read

want
good
catch
no
put

Read the Words

1. Max said, "I want a fish."

2. Fish are good to eat.

3. Will Max catch a fish?

4. No fish bit.

5. We put the fish in a pan.

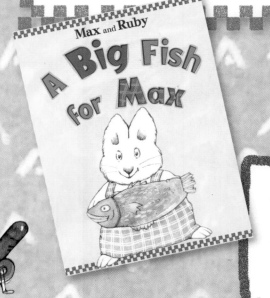

Genre: Animal Fantasy
An animal fantasy is a story with animals that act like humans. Next you will read about Max and Ruby—rabbits that go fishing.

Max and Ruby

A Big Fish for Max

written and designed by
Rosemary Wells

illustrated
by Jody Wheeler

Where will Max
get a big fish?

"I wish I had a fish to eat," said Max.

"Then we will catch a big fish,"
said Grandma.

"We can walk to the park," said Ruby.

"And Max will catch a big fish."

"Good," said Max. "Yum, yum, yum!"

The path in the park led to the pond.

"Max can fish in this pond," said Ruby.

Max sat.

He got a red ball in his net.

But no fish bit.

Then Max got a black ship in his net.
But no fish bit.

And then Max got a clam shell
in his net.

"I want to call the fish," said Ruby.
"Then I can talk to the fish."
But still no fish bit.

"Well, we can all walk to the fish shop," said Grandma.
"And we can talk to the fish man."

The fish man had lots of fish in a box.
"We want a fresh fish," said Grandma.
"That fat fish is good."

At home, Grandma put the fish
in a hot pan.
Then Ruby put the fish in a dish.

"Yum, yum, yum!" said Max.

Think and Share

Talk About It Max, Ruby, and Grandma care about each other. Find and read one part of the story that shows caring.

1. Use the pictures below to retell the story.

2. What was this story mostly about?

3. As you read, did you predict that Max would catch a fish? Find the part of the story that shows whether you were right.

Test Practice

Look Back and Write Look back at pages 20–22. Max did not catch a fish. What did he catch? Write those things.

Meet the Author

Rosemary Wells

Ms. Wells says, "Some of my most pleasurable memories as a child were of fishing with my father. We used to catch snapper blues, and my mother cooked them in parsley and butter that night. Today fish is still one of my favorite things to eat."

When Rosemary Wells writes stories about Max and Ruby, she thinks about what her own two girls said and did when they were children.

Read other books by Rosemary Wells.

29

At Home

We all want to help.
This plant is no good.
We dig it up.

Dad puts pots on the shelf.

Mom cuts the grass.

Sis can catch Gus.
We talk and have fun.

Nouns

· ·

A **noun** names a person, a place, an animal, or a thing.

· ·

The word **man** names a person.

The word **park** names a place.

The word **fish** names an animal.

The word **net** names a thing.

34

Write Using Nouns

1. Write the three things Max got in his net. Their names are nouns.

· ·

2. What place did Max, Ruby, and Grandma visit? Write a sentence about it. Draw a line under each noun.

· ·

3. What did Max do to get a fish? Write the steps he took. Draw a line under each noun you use.

Let's Talk About

People in Communities

Words to Read

could
be
old
paper
horse

Read the Words

1. Dave could be the pig in the class play.

2. Beth has an old hat for the play.

3. The class made paper masks.

4. Jake made a horse mask.

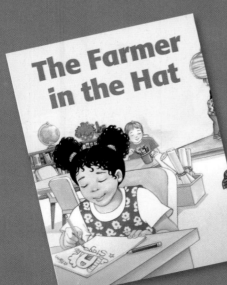

Genre: Realistic Fiction
Realistic fiction has characters that act like real people. You will read a story about classmates putting on a play.

The Farmer in the Hat

by Pat Cummings

Beth

Dave

Grace

Who will be the farmer in the play?

Max

Jake

Meg

"I have the hat. I could be the farmer, Old MacDonald, in this play," said Beth.

"No, I will be the
farmer," said Dave.

"You can be a pig," said Beth.
"A pig!" Dave made a face.

Grace went up on the stage. "We could make paper masks," she said. "Ducks, hens, a pig, a horse!"

"I have the hat!" said Max.
"I will be Old MacDonald,
not Beth!"

"Let me have that hat!" Dave said.

"Stop!" said Grace. "We must make masks."

Old MacDonald
★ Hens = Beth and Grace
★ Pig = Dave
★ Duck = Max
★ Farmer = ?

Max made a duck on his page.
Beth made hens.

Dave made a pig mask on his page.

"That is one odd pig," Grace said.

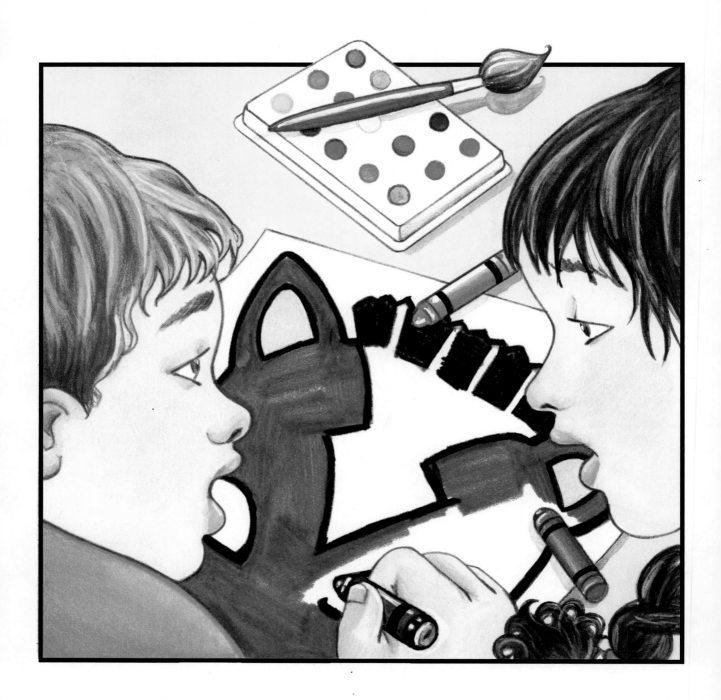

"It takes ages to make this horse mask," said Jake.

"I can make my mask fast," said Meg.

She made a fat gerbil mask.

"Place that gerbil in a paper cage,"
Jake said with a grin.

"Take your places up on the stage," said Grace.

"Grunt!" Dave had on his pig mask.

"Squeak!" said Meg.

"Quack!" Max had on his duck mask.

"Cluck." Beth had on her hen mask.

"Look at the cat!" said Grace.
"That is one odd farmer!"

Think and Share

Talk About It The author wrote a funny story about a class play. Read your favorite part of the story.

1. Use the pictures below to retell the story.

2. Why did the children forget about the farmer's hat?

3. The pictures give a clue about how the story will end. What clues do you see?

Look Back and Write Look back at the story. List the animals that will be in the play.

Pat Cummings

Pat Cummings once played a rabbit in a school play, and her sister played a grasshopper. Ms. Cummings made the cat the farmer in this story because "cats seem to naturally find the center of attention."

Ms. Cummings loves writing children's books. "The best part is that I can explore almost any subject."

Read two more books by Pat Cummings.

Helping Hands at 4-H

by Lindy Russell

Where could you see what farmers do? At a 4-H club!

How old are kids in 4-H? They can be ages 8 to 18.

At 4-H you can take care of
a horse or a pig.

You can get the eggs from the hens.

This 4-H club has a bake sale.
They place an ad in the paper.
They sell eggs too.

Bake Sale

Eggs
$ 2.00

The sale is good!
The club will get chicks.

The chicks will get big.
Then the club will have lots
of eggs to sell.

Proper Nouns

Special names for people, places, animals, and things are called **proper nouns.** Proper nouns begin with capital letters.

Max took the hat from **B**eth.

Max and **B**eth are proper nouns. They tell the names of a girl and a boy. **M**ax and **B**eth begin with capital letters.

Write Using Proper Nouns

1. Pick three children from the story. Their names are proper nouns. Write their names.

· ·

2. Your name and your friend's name are proper nouns. Write a sentence using your name and a friend's name. Did you use capital letters?

· ·

3. Could you make a mask for Old MacDonald? How would you do it? Write the steps. Use capital letters for proper nouns.

Let's Talk About
People in Communities

Mayor Sterling

Commonwealth
1800 N   Av

POLICE

65

Words to Read

| people |
| live |
| work |
| who |
| out |

Read the Words

1. People live here.

2. People work here too.

3. Who works here?

4. Who puts out fires?

Genre: Nonfiction

Nonfiction tells about real people and events. Next you will read about real people who live and work in a neighborhood.

Who Works

Who works where you live?

Here?

by Melissa Blackwell Burke
illustrated by Tim Spransy

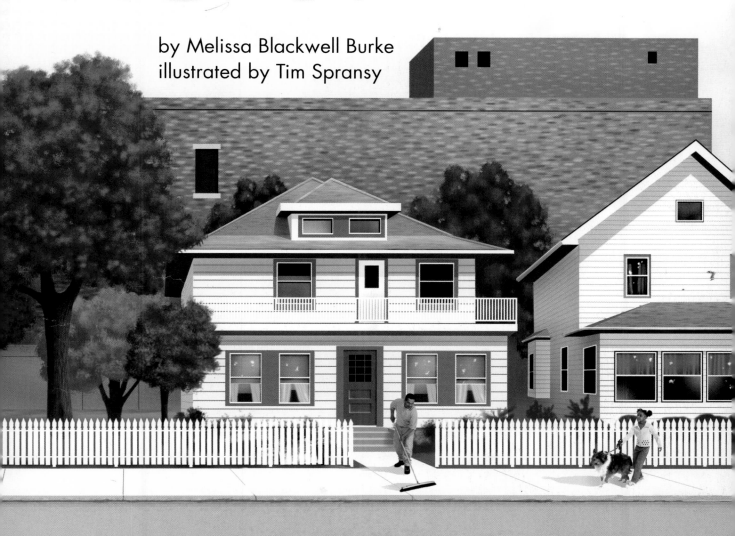

People live and work
in this neighborhood.
It is such a busy place.

Who works in this place?
We will talk to them.
They all like to help us.

71

I make the neighborhood safe.
When you ride your bike,
stop and check all ways.
I will help you cross.

I help put out fires. Fire can be bad.
I wish all people could be safe
from fire.

I put mail in your box.
People stop and wave and smile.
They like to chat a while.

I drive a big bus.
People can ride this bus to work.
I stop and pick them up.

I pick up trash.
When people put it out,
I pitch it in this truck.

76

Who works where you live?
Smile at them.
You will like them!

Think and Share

Talk About It *Who Works Here?* is about workers in a community. Tell about the job that interests you the most.

1. Use the pictures below to summarize what you learned.

2. What important information did the author want you to know?

3. Did anything confuse you? What question did you ask yourself as you read?

Look Back and Write Look back at page 77. What does this worker do?

Meet the Author

Melissa Blackwell Burke

Melissa Blackwell Burke grew up in a small town in Texas. She loved to visit the library. She says, "When I was a little girl, I wanted to be many things, including a teacher, a newspaper reporter, and a librarian. I have been two of those—a teacher and a newspaper reporter. Who knows—I might still become a librarian some day!"

Read other books about neighborhood workers.

Neighborhood Map

Use this map to check out where people live and work in this busy neighborhood.

- Who works on Pine Lane?

- Who works on Park Drive?

- Where is the bus stop?

- Where can you get stamps?

- Where is the truck that picks up the trash?

White Lane

Elm Drive

Park Drive

Pine Lane

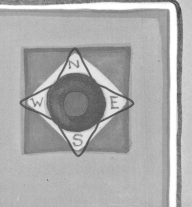

Read Together

Special Titles

A **title** can come before the name of a person. A title begins with a capital letter. Some titles end with a **period(.)**.

Officer Black helps me cross the street.

Ms. Timms brings us letters.

Dr. Vann is a vet.

Officer, Ms., and **Dr.** are special titles. Each begins with a capital letter. The titles **Ms.** and **Dr.** end with periods.

Write Using Special Titles

1. Make up names for some of the workers in *Who Works Here?* Write their names using special titles with capital letters and periods.

2. Write a sentence about someone who works in your neighborhood. Use capital letters and periods for special titles.

3. How does your teacher start your school day? Write about it. Use capital letters and periods for special titles.

Let's Talk About
Communities
in Nature

Words to Read

| there |
| down |
| inside |
| now |
| together |

Read the Words

1. I smell a baby there.

2. T. Rex ran up the slope and down.

3. The small animals went inside the circle.

4. Now T. Rex couldn't get his lunch.

5. They like being together.

Genre: Fiction

Fiction stories are made-up stories. Next you will read a made-up story about dinosaurs that lived a long time ago.

The Big Circle

by Eric Kimmel

illustrated by Richard Bernal

Who lived here long ago?

Big T. Rex wakes up.
Now Big T. Rex wants to eat,
but not bones and not stones.

Big T. Rex wants meat to eat.

Here is a herd of triceratops.
They are going home.

There they can get good grass to munch. The grass at home will make them fat.

Sniff, sniff. "Hmm," said Big T. Rex. "My nose smells a baby there. I'm good at hunting. I'll get that baby. It will make a good lunch."

Big T. Rex rose up on his back legs. He ran up the slope and down. The herd saw T. Rex run up and down.

They had time to make a big circle.
The small animals went inside the
circle. The baby went inside too.

Big T. Rex didn't like this.
Now he couldn't get his lunch.

But T. Rex didn't quit. "I'll make that herd run," he said.

But the herd didn't run.
They kept still in the big circle.

Then they gave T. Rex a poke and a bump. Together they drove him back.

Big T. Rex ran back up the slope and down. Those triceratops saw T. Rex run. Now they are safe.

They are going home to munch grass. Big T. Rex can't get them now. They like being together.

Think and Share

Talk About It The author wrote an exciting story about dinosaurs. Which part of the story did you like best? Why?

1. Use the pictures below to retell the story.

2. What happened after the triceratops saw Big T. Rex?

3. As you read the story, did anything confuse you? What did you do?

Look Back and Write Look back at the selection. Write about how the triceratops protect the baby.

Meet the Author and the Illustrator
Eric Kimmel

As a boy Eric Kimmel visited the Museum of Natural History in New York City almost every weekend. "The dinosaur skeletons were old friends," he says. "Triceratops and stegosaurus were my favorites."

Richard Bernal

Richard Bernal drew the pictures for this story. "I love dinosaurs," he says. "I have several dinosaur toys in my studio."

Read other books by Eric Kimmel and Richard Bernal.

Class Paper

Ms. Bell and Class Take Trip

Big Bones

Ms. Bell and her class went on a trip. They saw bones from a T. Rex.

They saw bones from
a triceratops. There aren't
animals like this now.

Cave Men

The class sat down and saw a film telling of cave men. Cave men went inside caves to live. They went hunting together.

Ms. Bell said, "I'm glad we went on this trip. We'll take many trips like this."

Days, Months, and Holidays

Days of the week, **months** of the year, and **holidays** all begin with capital letters.

Big T. Rex woke up on **Saturday.**

The triceratops went home to munch grass in **March.**

Mother's Day is next **Sunday.**

Write Using Days, Months, and Holidays

1. When is your birthday? Write the month. Look at a calendar. On what day of the week is your birthday this year? Write the day. Use capital letters.

· ·

2. Write a sentence about your favorite month. Be sure to use capital letters correctly.

· ·

3. What if there were a Dinosaur's Day? Tell two things you could do to celebrate this holiday.

Let's Talk About
Communities
in Nature

Words to Read

grow
food
around
find
water
under

Read the Words

1. The sun helps plants and trees grow.

2. Plants are good food for insects.

3. Birds look around to find insects to eat.

4. Water makes logs damp.

5. Grubs live under rocks and logs.

Genre: Expository Nonfiction
Expository nonfiction tells facts about real places. Next you will read about the plants and animals in a forest.

Life in the Forest

by Claire Daniel

What lives in the forest?

We can find life all around the forest.
It is a busy place!

The sun helped
these leaves
grow wide and flat.

Sun shines on the leaves
and helps them grow.
Many bugs like eating leaves.
Yum, yum! The bugs eat and eat.

A woodpecker sits on a branch.
Peck! Peck! Peck!
The woodpecker pecks for bugs.

These holes tell us that a woodpecker has pecked on this tree.

This huge log is soft and damp.
Water has made the log rot.
Small bugs made a home in the log.

This bird hops on the log
and pecks at it. Yum, yum!
It gets bugs from the log.

Nuts grow on trees and then fall all around. Squirrels find the nuts and eat them.

A fox is cute, but it likes to catch small animals like squirrels.

The black bear eats leaves, grass, and nuts. It likes grubs too. Grubs are small bugs under rocks and logs.

This bear looked for grubs under these rocks.

A hummingbird uses its bill to get food from this plant.

Many plants have shapes like tubes. Small hummingbirds like to sip food and water from these plants.

Hummingbirds can catch bugs for food too.

The forest is filled with life.
Many animals and plants call it home.
It is a busy place!

Think and Share

Talk About It Tell what you learned about the forest that you didn't know before.

1. Use the pictures below to summarize what you learned about life in the forest.

2. Why do you think the author wrote *Life in the Forest?*

3. What did you do to get ready to read *Life in the Forest?* How did that help you?

Look Back and Write Look back at pages 124–125. What do the squirrel and the fox eat?

Meet the Author
Claire Daniel

Claire Daniel learned about forests on a three-month hiking trip with her husband. "That was an amazing experience—being in the forest and living in it."

A bear came to their campsite once. "We heard him coming, so we ran to a shelter. It was a frightening experience! The bear went into our tent and then backed out of it, not finding any food."

Read more books by Claire Daniel.

A Mangrove

Have you watched fish
swim under a tree?

You can find fish in this forest.

These trees grow in salt water.

Fish swim under the trees.

Forest

by Terry Lynk
illustrated by Russell Farrell

Lots of animals live here.

Some live in the water.

Some live out of the water.

They are all around this forest.

Fish find food in the water.
Birds can use fish
and bugs as food.

But some forests like this are being lost. We must save these forests.

One and More Than One

Many nouns add **-s** to mean more than one.

● **nut + s = nuts** ●●
bug + s = bugs

This bear looked for **grubs** under these **rocks.**

The bear is looking for more than one grub. It is looking under more than one rock.

136

Write Using One and More Than One

1. Pick three forest animals from *Life in the Forest.* Write the words that name them. Then write the words again to show more than one.

. . . .

2. Write a sentence telling what squirrels eat. Use **-s** to show more than one.

. . . .

3. How do woodpeckers get their food? Write about what they eat and how they get it. Use **-s** to show more than one.

Let's Talk About

Communities in Nature

Words to Read

family

other

also

their

some

new

140

Read the Words

1. The queen bee rules the bee family.

2. Other bees also live in the hive.

3. These bees do their jobs well.

4. Some bees will make a new hive.

Genre: Expository Nonfiction

Expository nonfiction tells facts about real people, places, or animals. This article tells about honey bees.

Honey Bees

Honey Bees

by Jesús Cervantes

illustrated by Tom Leonard

What happens
inside a bee hive?

The sun shines. The honey bees wake
up. It is time for these insects to work.

Buzz,
buzz,
buzz.

In the hive, bees live together
like a family. In the family, there
is a queen bee, many worker
bees, and some drones.

This is the <u>queen</u> <u>bee</u>.
<u>She</u> rules the hive.

These are the drones.
They help the <u>queen</u>.

Their hive is hidden in a tree.
Worker bees keep this hive safe.

It is not good to make bees mad!
Bees will attack.

Worker bees make wax cells in the hive. These wax cells are small holes.

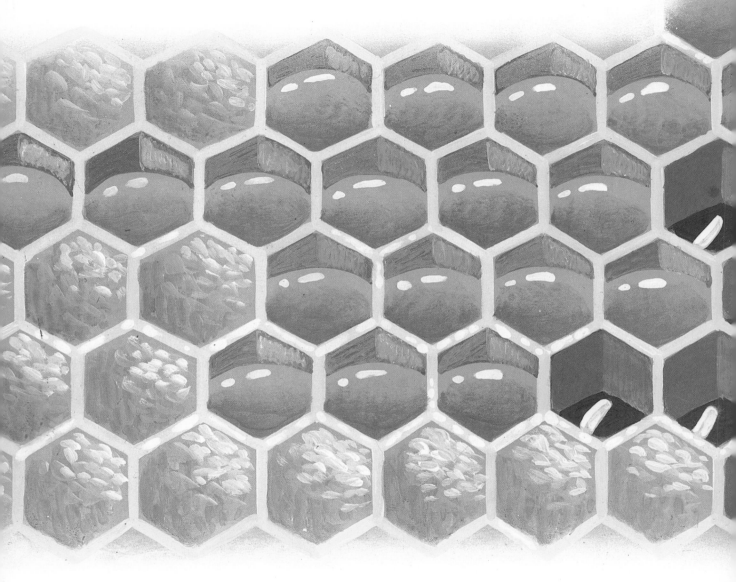

Bees save honey in some wax cells. Little bees live and grow in other cells.

Honey is food for bees.
Worker bees feed honey to
other bees in the hive. Bees
make honey from nectar.

Bees get nectar from flowers.
Honey bees find flowers with sweet
nectar. They take this sweet nectar
back inside their hive.

Worker bees also get pollen from flowers.

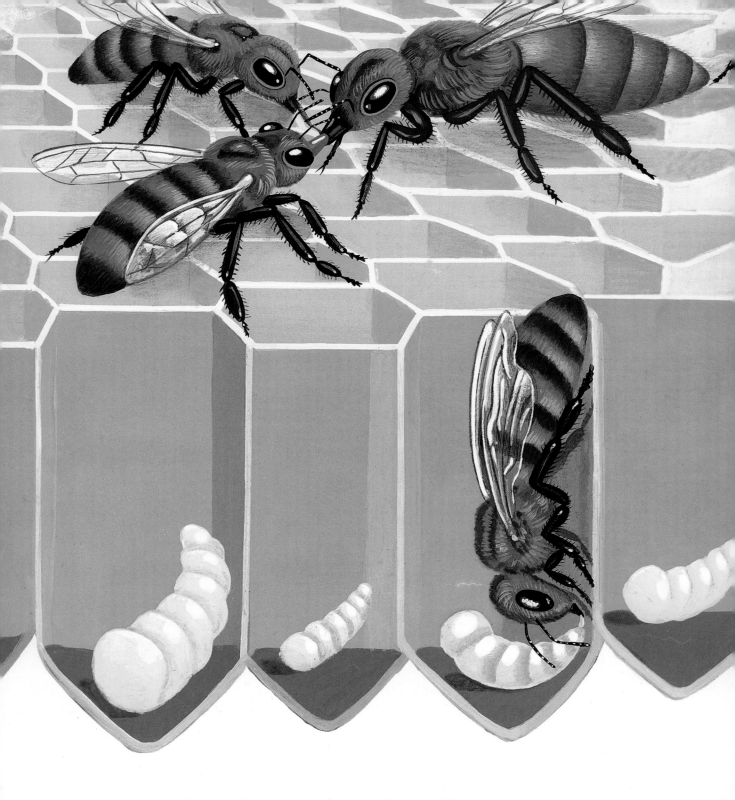

Worker bees feed pollen to
the queen bee and the little bees.
It helps them grow big.

When those little bees get big,
it is time for a new hive.

Worker bees make the new hive.
A new queen will also go with them.

When it gets cold, the bees
will go inside their hive to
sleep and rest. The bees will
wake up when the sun shines.

Think and Share

Talk About It Worker bees are very busy. What do you think is their most important job? Read the part that tells about it.

1. Use the pictures below to tell what you learned about honey bees.

2. How are a queen bee and a worker bee alike? How are they different?

3. What question did you have about bees before reading? How did that help you?

Look Back and Write What kinds of bees live in a hive? Look back at page 146.

Meet the Author
Jesús Cervantes

Jesús Cervantes grew up on a lemon and avocado ranch in southern California. He says, "The ranch had lots of bees. They were brought in to pollinate the trees. I wasn't afraid of bees when I was growing up."

Mr. Cervantes thinks bees are great. He says, "I love honey when it's still on the comb."

Read more about bees.

The Ants Go Marching

The ants go marching one by one,
Hurrah, hurrah.
The ants go marching one by one,
Hurrah, hurrah.
The ants go marching one by one,
The little one stops to have some fun.

And they all go marching down,
To the ground,
To get out
Of the rain.
BOOM! BOOM! BOOM! BOOM!

illustrated by Norman Gorbaty

161

Nouns in Sentences

A **noun** names a person, place, animal, or thing. A noun can be in more than one place in a sentence.

Their **hive** is hidden in a **tree.**

Both **hive** and **tree** are nouns. **Hive** is in the naming part of the sentence. **Tree** is in the action part of the sentence.

Write Using Nouns in Sentences

1. Write this sentence. Circle all of the nouns.

The bees will feed the queen.

· ·

2. Write a sentence that tells what bees get from flowers. Circle the nouns in your sentence.

· ·

3. How does the queen bee get her food? Write about it. Circle the nouns you use.

Wrap-Up

Thanks for the Help

connect to
WRITING

In this unit, you read about many different communities. Think of people in your community who help you every day. Write a thank-you letter to one of these people. Draw a picture of this person.

Dear Mail Carrier,
Thank you for bringing me letters. You do a good job.

Your pal,
Matt

Flower Power

The hummingbirds in *Life in the Forest* and the bees in *Honey Bees* both need flowers. Draw a picture that shows how bees and hummingbirds use flowers. Then write a caption that tells about your picture.

Make a Chart

You have read six stories about communities. Which did you like best? Which did your classmates like? Take a vote. Make a chart with the story titles. Mark a line to show each vote. Give the story with the most votes a star.

Stories	Votes
A Big Fish for Max	III
The Farmer in the Hat	III
Who Works Here?	I
⭐ The Big Circle	IIII
Life in the Forest	II
Honey Bees	III

Pictionary

My Family

mom
mama
mother
mommy

dad
papa
father
daddy

sister
daughter

This is me!

These are my relatives.

son
brother

uncle

cousin

aunt

baby

grandma
grandmother

grandpa
grandfather

Pictionary

My School

chalkboard

map

chalk

teacher

books

computer

ruler

eraser

pencil

scissors

clock

flag

bulletin board

student

crayon

table

lunchbox

chair

school

playground

cafeteria

classroom

169

Pictionary

Where People Live

houseboat

pueblo

log cabin

mobile home

high-rise

house

apartment building

townhouse

Pictionary

Where Animals Live

anthill

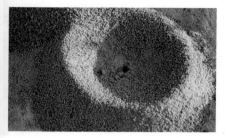

nest

hive

cave

den

log

barn

burrow

ocean

lodge

Pictionary

My Town

school

grocery store

bus driver

post office

crossing guard

mail carrier

garbage collector

173

Tested Words

Max and Ruby:
A Big Fish for Max

catch
good
no
put
want

The Farmer in
the Hat

be
could
horse
old
paper

Who Works Here?

live
out
people
who
work

The Big Circle

down
inside
now
there
together

Life in the Forest

around
find
food
grow
under
water

Honey Bees

also
family
new
other
some
their

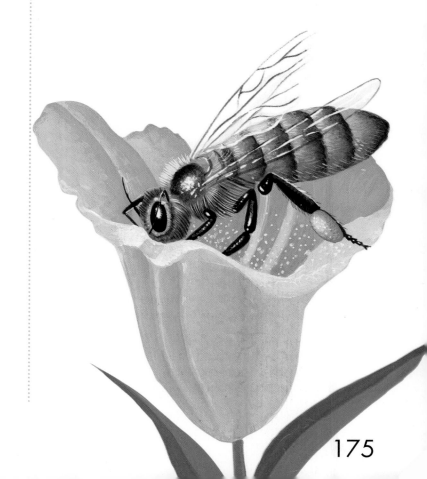

Acknowledgments

Illustrations

Cover: Daniel Moreton

8, 164 Mark Buehner

11-35 Jody Wheeler

38 Pat Cummings

68-77 Tim Spransy

74-75 April Mosakowski Hartmann

78-102 Richard Bernal

132-135 Russell Farrell

138 Amy Vangsgard

142-157 Tom Leonard

144 Norman Gorbaty

172 Stephen Lewis

Photographs

Every effort has been made to secure permission and provide appropriate credit for photographic material. The publisher deeply regrets any omission and pledges to correct errors called to its attention in subsequent editions.

Unless otherwise acknowledged, all photographs are the property of Scott Foresman, a division of Pearson Education.

Photo locators denoted as follows: Top (T), Center (C), Bottom (B), Left (L), Right (R), Background (Bkgd).

9 ©Bill Ross/Corbis

10 ©Gabe Palmer/Corbis

11 (T) ©Tom & Dee Ann McCarthy/Corbis, (BL) ©Sean Justice/Getty Images, (CR) ©Britt Erlanson/Getty Images

36 ©Ariel Skelley/Corbis

37 (TL) ©LWA-Dann Tardif/Corbis, (BL) ©Tom & Dee Ann McCarthy/Corbis, (TR) ©Gabe Palmer/Corbis

57, 58 Wagner Farm, Glenview Park District, Glenview, IL.

60 (CR, CL) ©G K & Vikki Hart/Getty Images

61 ©Melanie Acevedo/FoodPix

64 Getty Images

65 (T) ©Patrick Ward/Corbis, (BL) ©Michael Newman/PhotoEdit

84 ©Stephen Wilkes/Getty Images

85 (T) ©Paul Souders/Getty Images, (BL) ©Stephen Frink/Corbis

113 ©Royalty-Free/Corbis

114 ©Naturfoto Honal/Corbis

115 ©Steve Kaufman/Corbis

116 ©Bill Ross/Corbis

117 (TR) Photowood Inc./Corbis, (TL) Steve Kaufman/Corbis, (CL, BR) ©Royalty-Free/Corbis

118 (C) ©Photowood Inc./Corbis, (BL) ©Tom Uhlman/Visuals Unlimited

119 ©Steve Kaufman/Corbis

120 ©Naturfoto Honal/Corbis

121 ©Fritz Polking/Visuals Unlimited

122 ©Jamie Harron/Papilio/Corbis

124 ©Stephen Dalton/Photo Researchers, Inc.

125 (TR) ©Gerard Fuehrer/Visuals Unlimited, (B) Getty Images

126 (T) ©Jim Clare/Nature Picture Library

127 (T) ©Frederick D. Atwood

128 (Bkgd) ©Bill Ross/Corbis, (BR) ©Royalty-Free/Corbis, (TR) ©Melissa Farlow/Aurora & Quanta Productions, (CL) ©Gary W. Carter/Corbis, (TL) ©Bill Dyer/Photo Researchers, Inc.

129 (TL) ©Stephen Krasemann/Getty Images, (BR) ©Tim Thompson/Corbis

131 ©John Kreis Photography

135 ©Theo Allofs/Danita Delimont, Agent

136 Getty Images

137 ©Stephen Dalton/Photo Researchers, Inc.

138 (BC) ©Ewing Galloway/Index Stock Imagery, (CR) ©Tim Laman/NGS Image Collection

139 (TL) ©Karen Moskowitz/Getty Images, (CC) © Colombini Medeiros, Fabio/Animals Animals/Earth Scenes

168 ©Tim Ridley/DK Images

169 (CR) ©Richard Orton/Index Stock Imagery, (BCR) ©Mary Kate Denny/PhotoEdit, (TR) ©David R. Frazier/Photolibrary, Inc./Alamy Images, (BR) ©Ed Bock/Corbis

170 (TL) ©Jan Butchofsky-Houser/Corbis, (TR) ©E. R. Degginger/Color-Pic, Inc., (BCL) ©Royalty-Free/Corbis, (CC) ©Richard Bickel/Corbis, (BC) ©Kim Sayer/Corbis, (TCL) ©Tony Perrottet/Omni Photo Communications, (BL) Getty Images, (BR) ©John Coletti/DK Images

171 (BR) ©Steve Shott/DK Images, (BL) ©Douglas Peebles/Corbis, (TR) ©Karen Moskowitz/Getty Images, (BC) ©Roger Leo/Index Stock Imagery, (CC) ©Stouffer Productions/Animals Animals/Earth Scenes, (TC) ©Frank Greenaway/Courtesy of the National Prey Centre, Cloucestershire/DK Images, (BCL, TL, CL) Getty Images, (CR) ©Fritz Polking/Visuals Unlimited, (TR) ©Frank Greenaway/DK Images

Glossary

The contents of this glossary have been adapted from *First Dictionary*. Copyright ©2000, Pearson Education, Inc.

Reading STREET

Grade **1**

Reading/Language Arts

Tennessee
Reading and Writing Accomplishments

Reading Accomplishments
Content Standard 1.0

The student will develop the reading and listening skills necessary for word recognition, comprehension, interpretation, analysis, evaluation, and appreciation of print and nonprint text.

1.1.01   Develop oral language.

a.   Show evidence of expanding oral language through vocabulary growth.

b.   Implement rules for conversation (e.g., raise hands, take turns, focus attention on speaker).

c.   Understand, follow, and give oral directions.

d.   Participate in group discussions.

e.   Participate in creative responses to text (e.g., choral reading, discussion, and drama).

f.   Respond to questions from teacher and other group members.

g.   Begin to narrate a personal story.

h.   Dramatize or retell what has been learned, heard, or experienced.

i.   Use familiar texts for recitations.

1.1.02   **Develop listening skills.**

     a.   Listen attentively to speaker for specific information.

     b.   Use appropriate listening skills (e.g., do not interrupt, face speaker, ask questions).

     c.   Listen and respond to a variety of media (e.g., books, audio tapes, videos).

     d.   Recognize the difference between formal and informal languages.

     e.   Understand and follow simple, three-step oral directions.

1.1.03   **Demonstrate knowledge of concepts of print.**

     a.   Understand that printed materials provide information.

     b.   Demonstrate directionality by reading left to right and top to bottom.

     c.   Track print when being read to aloud.

     d.   Read and explain own writings and drawings.

     e.   Identify parts of a book (e.g., title page, table of contents).

     f.   Recognize that groups of words make sentences.

     g.   Understand punctuation (e.g., period, question mark).

1.1.04   **Develop and maintain phonemic awareness.**

     a.   Recognize words that begin with the same sounds.

     b.   Recognize words that end with the same sounds.

     c.   Identify rhyming words.

     d.   Blend sounds together to form one-syllable words.

     e.   Segment one-syllable words into sounds.

     f.   Change targeted sounds to modify or change words.

     g.   Show awareness of syllables by clapping, counting, or moving objects.

1.1.05   Develop and use decoding strategies.

a. Use knowledge of letter-sound correspondence knowledge and structural analysis to decode grade-appropriate words.

b. Decode phonetically regular, one-syllable words.

c. Use decoding strategies, such as sounding out words, comparing similar words, breaking words into smaller words, and looking for word parts (e.g., compound words, word families, blends, and digraphs).

d. Apply long and short vowel rules when decoding.

e. Begin to decode unknown words automatically.

1.1.06   Read to develop fluency, expression, accuracy, and confidence.

a. Begin to read orally with accuracy and confidence using appropriate pacing, intonation, and expression.

b. Reflect punctuation of written text while reading orally.

c. Participate in guided oral readings.

d. Demonstrate the automatic recognition of high-frequency words.

e. Read with increasing fluency and confidence from a variety of texts through paired readings, shared reading, choral reading, teacher-led reading, and reading from tapes.

f. Read independently daily.

g. Recite familiar texts to develop fluency, expression, accuracy, and confidence.

1.1.07   **Develop and extend reading vocabulary.**

    a.   Build vocabulary by listening to literature, participating in discussions, and reading self-selected texts.

    b.   Build vocabulary through frequent read alouds.

    c.   Participate in shared reading.

    d.   Manipulate word families, word walls, and word sorts.

    e.   Match oral words to written words.

    f.   Determine the meaning of unfamiliar words by using a picture dictionary, picture clues, context clues, and structural analysis.

    g.   Add endings to base words (e.g., *-s, -ed, -es, -ing*).

    h.   Identify simple abbreviations.

1.1.08   **Develop and use prereading strategies.**

    a.   Develop a purpose for listening/reading.

    b.   Participate in activities to build background knowledge to derive meaning from text.

    c.   Make predictions about text.

    d.   Use illustrations to preview text.

1.1.09 **Use active comprehension strategies to derive meaning while reading and check for understanding after reading.**

    a.   Derive meaning while reading by

        1.   asking questions about text.

        2.   recognizing errors in reading as they occur and self-correct.

        3.   participating in discussions about text and relating to personal experiences.

        4.   creating graphic organizers (e.g., charts, lists).

        5.   predicting and adjusting outcomes during read alouds.

    b.   Check for understanding after reading by

        1.   recalling three- to four-step sequence of events.

        2.   retelling stories in their own words using sequencing words (i.e. *first, next, last*).

        3.   drawing conclusions based on what has been read.

        4.   recognizing main idea in pictures, picture books, and texts.

1.1.10 **Introduce informational skills to facilitate learning.**

    a.   Recognize the family and community as sources of information.

    b.   Recognize a variety of print items as sources of information (e.g. books, magazines, maps, charts, and graphs).

    c.   Recognize sources of information (e.g., books, maps, graphs, charts).

    d.   Use graphic organizers to aid in understanding material from informational text (e.g., charts, graphs, web).

    e.   Visit libraries to use and view appropriate material.

1.1.11 **Develop skills to facilitate reading to learn in a variety of content areas.**

    a.   Begin to develop content-specific vocabulary.

    b.   Use text features to locate information (e.g., maps, charts, illustrations, and table of contents).

1.1.12 **Read independently for a variety of purposes. (At this level, the student will explore as an emergent reader.)**

    a.   Read for literary experience.

    b.   Read to gain information.

    c.   Read to perform a task.

    d.   Read for enjoyment.

    e.   Read to expand vocabulary.

    f.   Read to build fluency.

1.1.13 **Experience various literary and media genres.**

    a.   Read and view various literary (e.g., picture books, storybooks, fairy tales, poetry, lyrics to songs) and media (e.g., illustrations, the arts, films, videos) genres.

    b.   Explore nonfiction.

    c.   Identify characters, events, and settings in print and nonprint text.

    d.   Recognize main character(s) in print and nonprint text.

    e.   Determine whether a selection is real or fantasy.

    f.   Recognize rhyme in Mother Goose and other rhyming books.

    g.   Retell a story in correct sequence (e.g., using books, videos, films).

    h.   Determine the problem in a story and discover its solution through classroom discussion.

1.1.14 **Develop and maintain a motivation to read.**

    a.   Visit libraries/media centers and regularly check out materials.

    b.   Share storybooks, poems, newspapers, and environmental print.

    c.   Explore a wide variety of literature through read alouds, tapes, and independent reading.

    d.   Identify favorite stories, informational text, authors, and illustrators.

    e.   Engage in a variety of literacy activities voluntarily (e.g., self-select books and stories).

    f.   Choose to read as a leisure activity.

Writing Accomplishments
Content Standard 2.0

The student will develop the structural and creative skills of the writing process necessary to produce written language that can be read, presented to, and interpreted by various audiences.

1.2.01   **Use a variety of prewriting strategies.**

   a.   Brainstorm ideas with teacher and peers.

   b.   Draw pictures to generate ideas.

   c.   Construct graphic organizers (e.g., webs, charts, diagrams) as a small or large group to organize information.

   d.   Use a variety of sources to gather information.

1.2.02   **Write for a variety of purposes.**

   a.   Write to acquire and exhibit knowledge (e.g., word families, numbers, shapes, sensory words, and sentences).

   b.   Write to entertain (e.g., stories and poems).

   c.   Write to inform (e.g., write simple directions, journals, friendly letters).

1.2.03   **Show evidence of drafting and revision with written work.**

   a.   Compose first drafts using appropriate parts of the writing process with an emphasis on planning and self-correction.

   b.   Write in complete, coherent sentences.

   c.   Use descriptive words when writing.

   d.   Use temporary spelling to spell independently as necessary.

   e.   Arrange events in logical/sequential order when writing or dictating.

   f.   Participate in teacher-led experience stories.

   g.   Reread draft and delete extraneous information.

   h.   Vary sentence types.

1.2.04   Include editing before the completion of finished work.

a. Apply elements of language (e.g., end marks, capitalization) and use complete sentences when writing and editing.

b. Use classroom resources (e.g., word walls, picture dictionaries, teacher, peers, appropriate technology, student-generated word books) to support the writing process.

c. Use knowledge of letter sounds, word parts, and word segmentation to monitor and correct spelling.

d. Create readable documents with legible handwriting.

e. Identify words or phrases that could be added to clarify meaning after writing or dictating a story.

1.2.05   Evaluate own and others' writing.

a. Use a simple rubric to evaluate writing/pictures and group work (e.g., happy face, stickers).

b. Discuss and react to writing.

c. Review personal collection to determine progress.

1.2.06   Experience numerous publishing opportunities.

a. Prepare a variety of written work (e.g., published books, classroom books, experience stories).

b. Use technology to publish writing.

c. Share completed work.

d. Create individual and classroom books.

e. Incorporate illustrations and photographs.

1.2.07   Write narrative accounts.

a. Write simple stories.

b. Write short accounts of personal experiences.

c. Write group stories with a beginning, middle, and ending.

1.2.08   **Write frequently across content areas.**

  a.   Summarize concepts presented in science (e.g., illustration, dictating sentences, or composing simple sentences).

  b.   Write stories using concepts presented in social studies.

  c.   Write in math journals, create math stories, and write explanations for problem solving.

  d.   Participate in shared writings about the arts and class activities.

1.2.09   **Write expressively using original ideas, reflections, and observations.**

  a.   Write when given time, place, and materials.

  b.   Maintain, with teacher assistance, samples of writing and drawings that express opinions and judgments (e.g., portfolio, journals, student-made books).

  c.   Dictate stories (e.g., to tape recorder, to adult, to older student).

1.2.10   **Write in response to literature.**

  a.   Write different endings to a story.

  b.   Summarize a story using simple sentences and illustrations.

  c.   Create class books based on literature selections.

  d.   Create and/or use an illustration, sign, or rebus symbols to respond to literature.

1.2.11   **Write in a variety of modes and genres.**

  a.   Write friendly notes and messages.

  b.   Write stories.

  c.   Write in journals.

  d.   Write rhymes and poems.

Elements of Language Accomplishments
Content Standard 3.0

The student will use standard English conventions and proper spelling as appropriate to speaking and writing.

1.3.01 **Demonstrate knowledge of standard English usage.**

a. Use nouns appropriately (e.g., singular and plural, possessive).

b. Use verbs (action words) appropriately (e.g., tense and agreement with simple subject).

c. Use pronouns appropriately (e.g., subject and object agreement).

d. Use adjectives appropriately (e.g., vivid description words).

1.3.02 **Demonstrate knowledge of standard English mechanics.**

a. Capitalize the first word of a sentence, first and last names, pronoun *I*, and proper nouns.

b. Use correct punctuation at the end of simple declarative sentences and questions.

c. Identify and use contractions.

d. Write legibly in manuscript, using proper spacing between letters of a word and words of a sentence.

1.3.03 **Demonstrate knowledge of standard English spelling.**

a. Spell high-frequency words correctly.

b. Spell words correctly as appropriate to grade level.

c. Spell three- and four-letter short vowel words and phonetically spell sight words correctly.

d. Alphabetize words to the first letter.

e. Begin to develop dictionary skills through the use of a picture dictionary.

1.3.04 Demonstrate knowledge of correct sentence structure.

a. Use complete and coherent sentences when speaking.

b. Identify complete sentences.

c. Write a simple sentence.

d. Identify and correct incomplete sentences.

e. Combine two simple sentences into a compound sentence using the word *and.*

f. Identify statements and questions by noting ending punctuation when writing and intonation when speaking.

Reading
STREET
Grade 1